GREAT MILITARY BLUNDERS

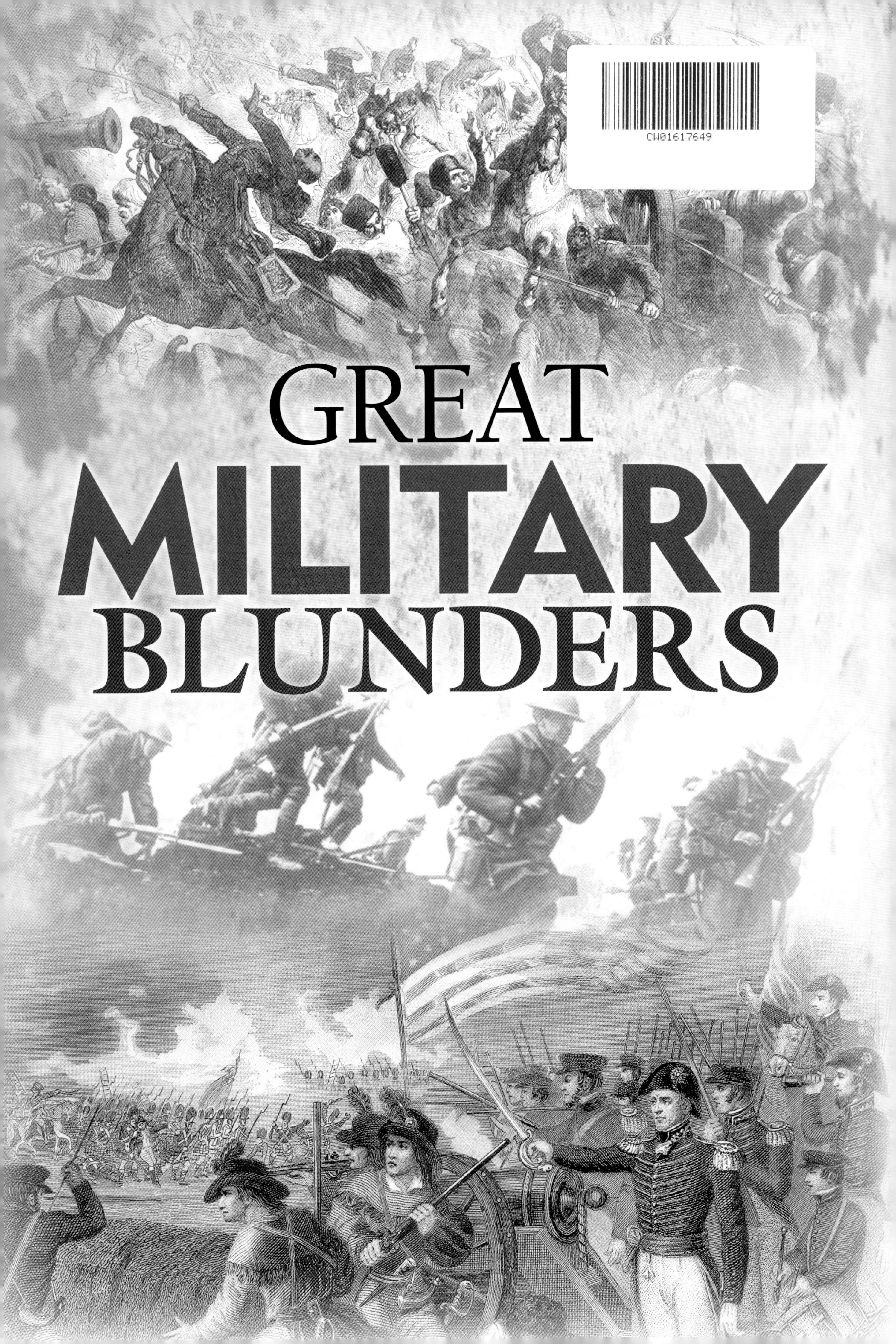

Contents

GREAT MILITARY BLUNDERS

First published in the UK in 2013

This edition published by Park Lane Books

www.parklanebooksltd.vpweb.co.uk

Printed in China

ISBN: 978-1-906969-26-4

Designed by: BrainWave

Creative Director: Kevin Gardner

Written by: Bill Lucas

Images courtesy of PA Photos, Imperial War Museum, Matt H Wade, Stephen Mckay, and Wiki Commons

Introduction

Not every defeat is a blunder, and equally not every victory is a demonstration of great skill and tactical brilliance. When two opposing forces face each other in battle, both having taken all sensible steps to ensure their best effort and outcome, it is inevitable that one side will prevail and the other will suffer defeat. Such an encounter requires no blunder – just an honest exchange.

A blunder denotes a specific decision, or failure, which should not have been made and upon which the enemy could never plan or rely.

There may be admirable qualities within the madness of conflict, but the vices of war are the vices of men – cowardice, vanity, cruelty, and stupidity – and we can discern traces of all of these as we sift through the archaeology of some of the most shocking military blunders in history.

However, nothing that we will find obscures the most important truth… the greatest blunder of all is war itself.

■ **RIGHT:** **US marines of the 28th Regiment of the Fifth Division raise the American flag atop Mount Suribachi, Iwo Jima, on February 23, 1945. Strategically located only 660 miles from Tokyo, the Pacific island became the site of one of the bloodiest, most famous battles of World War II against Japan.**

JOSEPH W
SMITH

HONOUR
THE FALLEN
AT THE
GOING DOWN
OF THE SUN AND
IN THE MORNING

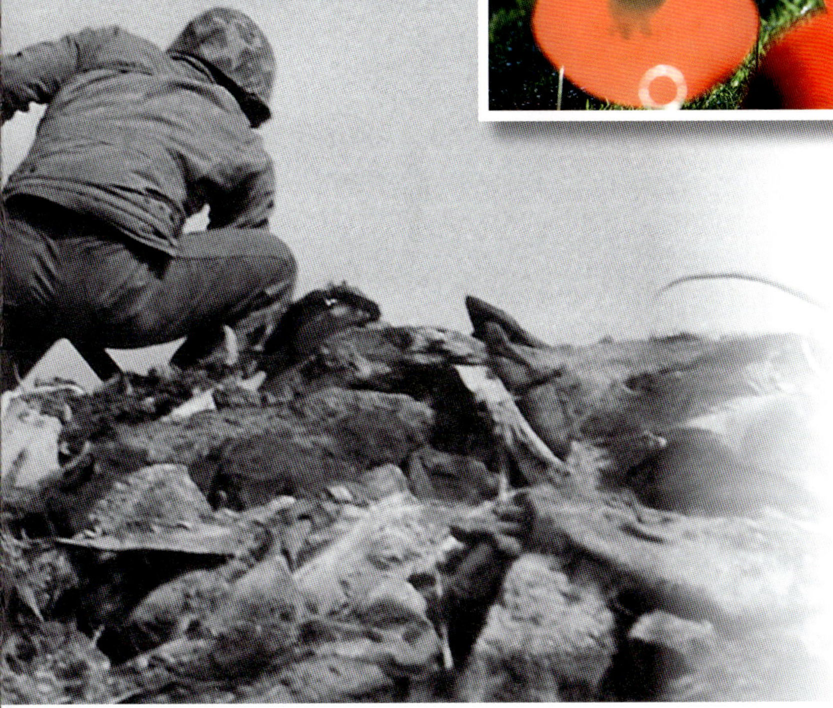

The Battle of Stirling Bridge

Throughout history one of the most common blunders made by military commanders has been to underestimate the enemy, and all too frequently nobles of high rank, when fighting those whom they regarded as the lower classes or savages, have made this error. Rarely has this fatal miscalculation been better executed than by John de Warenne in his action at Stirling Bridge on September 11, 1297, which, were it not for the dreadful loss of life and the suffering of so many, can almost appear farcical in its ineptitude.

In its war against Scottish independence the English army had achieved notable successes in the past and de Warenne had led his men to victory in the battle of Dunbar only a year before. Confident and full of swagger, he had not reckoned on the effect that William Wallace – commander of the Scots for only four months – would have upon the morale and prowess of his "savage" opponents.

Leading over 12,000 men, including up to 3,000 cavalry led by the aristocratic Hugh de Cressingham,

de Warenne decided to cross the Forth River close to Stirling Castle, fully aware that a Scottish force of less than 2,500 awaited him on the other side. He brought his men to a halt at the south of the river near to a small wooden bridge and waited for the Scots to surrender. This remained the position for three days as two friars were sent back and forth in parley, but Wallace and his ally Andrew Murray would have none of it.

De Warenne now had little choice but to attack, but the problem with an English advance was that the bridge was so narrow that only two horsemen could ride across it abreast, rendering the crossing of a large force extremely slow. The English commander was advised that, to defend this slow progress, a force of cavalry should be sent to cross at a ford further up the river, protecting his troops from a flanking attack. However, de Cressingham – who was also the English king's Treasurer in Scotland – dissuaded him from this action on financial grounds. And so it was, that at dawn the next morning, the English advanced across the bridge.

However, they were soon recalled, as de Warenne had overslept and was not ready. So, later in the morning, they set off again… only to be recalled once more as the commander thought that the Scots might still surrender. The friars were sent off again and returned with the final message from Wallace and Murray – "we are not here to make peace but to do battle, defend ourselves and liberate our kingdom. Let them come on…" – so on they came.

The long slow progress across the slender bridge, led by de Cressingham, took several hours and the Scottish forces let them come, waiting until 5,400 foot soldiers and over 200 cavalry had made the crossing, at which point they swept down, spears in hand. In preparation they had scattered caltrops – ragged twists of sharp metal – on the ground to disable the cavalry and the English force, now in disarray, was rapidly overcome. Some, who were able to strip off their armor, swam back to the southern shore.

De Warenne, left on the south of the river with still a huge force, ordered the destruction of the bridge and, ultimately, fled south. De Cressingham, his heavy cavalry, and thousands of foot soldiers, were massacred and his skin was stripped from his body and passed around in pieces as tokens of victory.

The English dead numbered 5,000 infantry and 100 cavalrymen.

ABOVE: The Wallace Monument.

BELOW: A statue of William Wallace.

The Battle of Agincourt

It was not known at the time of course, but in 1415 the grinding Hundred Years War between the English and French was only two-thirds through and several generations had never known peace. Indeed, many of the French soldiers, who were massing to meet the English

before they could reach their stronghold in Calais, had lost their grandfathers or fathers in earlier savage encounters, and memories of Crécy and Poitiers burned hot in their Gallic souls. They were hungry for a fight.

The English king, Henry, fifth of that name, was a charismatic 29-year-old who fought alongside his men and was much loved by his knights and men-at-arms alike. Having recently taken the important seaport of Harfleur, following a siege of longer duration than anticipated, Henry had decided to take his main force, seriously weakened by dysentery, to safety in the English-held Calais. Having left a small garrison in Harfleur, he set out with approximately 8,500 men toward the river Somme, leaving his artillery behind and taking only limited provisions.

The French army, commanded by Constable Charles d'Albret and growing stronger day by day, stalked and pressured the English and delayed an easy crossing – but eventually the river was crossed. By now Henry's forces had marched over 260 miles and were extremely short of food. D'Albret now chose to block the road to Calais to force a confrontation, while still awaiting further forces to add to his already huge army. It was here that the French commander made the first, and severest, of several blunders.

When the armies eventually faced each other, Henry's men were outnumbered by the French by at least four to one. They were also tired, sick, and hungry. The French, on the other hand, were well equipped, confident, and ready to give Henry a beating. However, d'Albret had chosen a dangerous spot to force the encounter. Between the opposing lines lay open ground recently ploughed and bordered on both sides by thick wooded terrain. The English dug in, planting sharpened stakes into the ground at an angle to defend against a cavalry charge. And the French hesitated.

D'Albret, despite his superior forces, still wanted to await reinforcements and, as a delaying

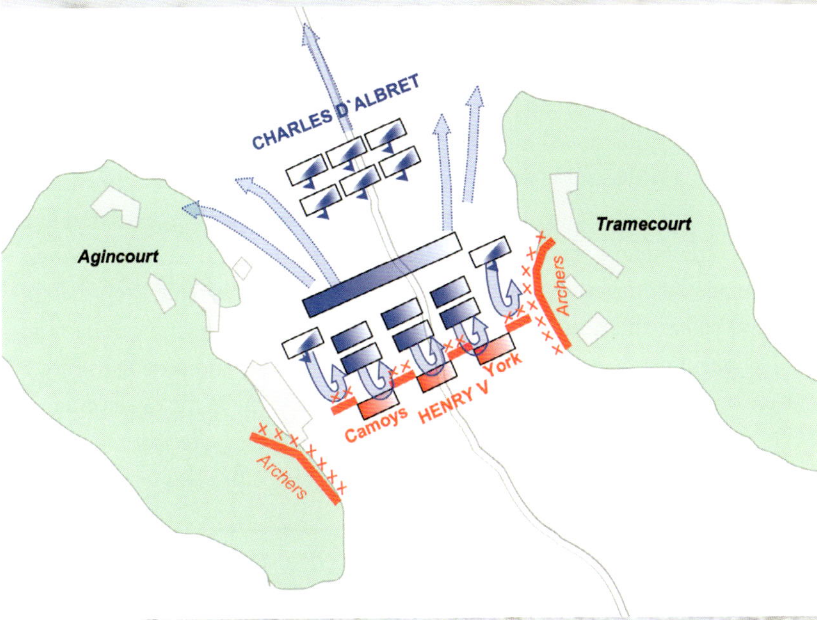

ABOVE: A map of the Agincourt battle.

BELOW: The morning of the Battle of Agincourt, by Sir John Gilbert.

tactic, opened negotiations with the English. Henry did not want to attack, as he knew that he would do better in a defensive action, but he took the opportunity to move his forces forward to decrease the gap. In so doing, he moved into the narrowest area between the woods on both sides, thus preventing flanking attacks by the French, but took a risk, as this maneuver meant uprooting his defensive stakes and re-siting them in his new position.

Here was d'Albret's second blunder. While the English were on the move the French cavalry was taking it easy, feeding the horses, or warming themselves up in recreation. Had they attacked before Henry's defensive stakes were replaced, it is probable that they would have overrun the English with relative ease. Instead, they continued to wait until eventually, Henry, now satisfied with the strength of his defensive position, opened hostilities with a huge volley of arrows from his longbowmen. The battle was on.

The French had established a battle plan placing their 4,000 archers and 1,500 crossbowmen in front of their vast number of men-at-arms but, unaccountably, after their first return volley, the archers were consigned to the rear behind the cavalry and heavily-armored knights who were pushing for pole position in their eagerness to fight.

Between Henry's men and this seething multitude lay a ploughed field, already much softened to mud by heavy rain. The French cavalry charged but immediately found the going tough, their massive weight pushing the horses' legs into the heavy earth. Hail upon hail of English arrows rained down on the slowly advancing horsemen and a previously unimaginable carnage began to unfold. Behind the first cavalry charge an immense force, sometimes estimated to be as many as 50,000 in number, hungered to attack and soon the first line of massively armored men-at-arms strode out into the affray on ground now churned by the sinking cavalry. Terrified horses turned and ran back through the on-coming French while English arrows continued to fall in torrents. The knights sunk deeper into the mud but, even so, the French second line was unleashed and all were pressed by uncontrollable forces from behind. The dead and dying in front became further hurdles and progress slowed by the moment as the crush from behind rendered effective movement impossible, with many French fighters unable to wield their weapons or even find an Englishman to fight.

On that day, October 25, 1415, by choosing a poor position, hesitation, and a lack of discipline, d'Albret suffered a massive defeat – one on such a scale that it altered the course of history. The final numbers are not clear, but it is known that the French lost between 4,000 and 10,000 men in the battle, while Henry's losses numbered less than 500 from his small and exhausted band of brothers.

As Shakespeare would later recount "... the fewer men, the greater share of honour."

BELOW: A portrait of King Henry V, King of England 1413-1422.

Equipment

Having the right equipment in sufficient quantity is a prerequisite for any successful military campaign. Much modern technology – such as radar – has its origins in equipment that was developed for the military, and many advances in medicine have occurred as a result of lessons learned on the battlefield. For the most part, given that much of the equipment used is at the cutting edge, it generally performs well, but there are numerous cases of soldiers being provided with equipment that was not fit for purpose.

Since 2001 NATO has been involved in a war against the Taliban in Afghanistan. Although the regime in Kabul was quickly toppled, for more than a decade the NATO force has been waging a war against guerrillas and insurgents. The same was equally true following the joint British/US invasion of Iraq in 2003 when, following the toppling of the regime of Saddam Hussein, the occupying forces faced an ever-present threat from militants and insurgents. For these irregular forces a weapon of choice is the Improvised Explosive Device (IED). These crude and homemade mines have been responsible for the killing of many foot soldiers as well as a large number of British soldiers traveling in supposedly safe vehicles. Although the British army has armored vehicles such as the Warrior, capable of resisting blast damage from IEDs, it chose to send troops on patrol using "snatch" Land Rovers that were ill-equipped to deal with such a threat. Following the death of a number of British soldiers, the British Ministry of Defence was sued over its duty of care to soldiers. The fatalities that resulted from the use of the "snatch" Land Rovers resulted in them being phased out after 2008.

It wasn't only the "snatch" Land Rover that proved a liability for British troops in Afghanistan. The Bowman radio system, which cost more than $3 billion to develop, was condemned as "astonishingly bad" by one officer. Sometimes, for example, shortages of batteries meant that soldiers were instructed to keep the radio switched off until they were actually under attack.

Soldiers, as all military men do, recognize that theirs is a hazardous occupation; equipment failure, however, is something that none can accept.

■ **LEFT & BELOW: Snatch Land Rover conversions.**

The Battle of Flodden Field

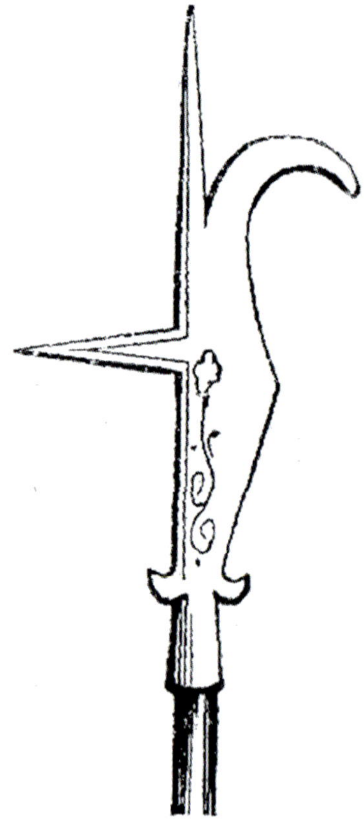

RIGHT: **The blade of the bill, sitting on a nine-foot-long pole.**
BELOW: **The site of the Battle of Flodden Field.**

The bloody battle at Flodden saw the greatest Scottish military defeat in history, the death of a king, and the slaughter of over 10,000 men, all in only a few hours. When it was over, the tattered remnants of the Scottish army limped home in shame. But what had gone so disastrously wrong that had caused the proud 36,000-strong Scottish army to be so soundly beaten by a much smaller English command? Much of the answer lies in the equipment used by the opposing forces... with the odd blunder or two thrown in for good measure.

As a result of Henry VIII's war with France, King James IV of Scotland lived up to his alliance with the French by declaring war on England. He raised an army, which included 5,000 French troops, and abandoned the traditional spear that the Scots had used for so long in favor of the Continental pike – a long sharpened pole – much used in Europe, frequently in defensive actions. Pulled together from a variety of sources and trained by foreigners, it is unlikely that his men were completely at ease with this new weapon as they crossed the border in August 1513. King James had his eye on taking the castle at Norham in Northumberland as his first conquest and took a number of heavy siege cannon with him as they trekked south. The guns proved to be perfect for pounding the heavily fortified castle and James succeeded in taking Norham in a few days.

Meanwhile, an English army, some 25,000 strong and led by Thomas Howard, Earl of Surrey, was making its way north to stop the Scottish advance. They were armed with the latest innovation in battlefield technology, the bill – a nine-foot-long pole topped with a scything blade that had a devastating cutting edge.

In a peculiarly gentlemanly way Howard sent a messenger offering battle with James on September 9, on a ground of equal advantage to both sides. Imagine his disgust then when, arriving on the field, he found that James had stationed his army up in the hills in a heavily defended position… this was not the battle that he had envisaged.

It was not feasible for Howard to attack the Scots in their commanding position and so, rather than withdraw, Howard decided to go around and outflank them. In order to do so he had to cross the River Till at Twizel Bridge and here James could have ended the English ambitions. Although probably shrouded in mist the English maneuver could have been stopped at the bridge by a small force with some light artillery… but James failed to react and the English were able to achieve a better offensive position on the north of the river.

At about 4pm James opened hostilities by using his cannon to bombard the English positions. However, the heavy siege artillery was ill-suited to this purpose and could not be sufficiently depressed in elevation to cause much damage to the enemy. Meanwhile, Howard's 22 guns, much lighter and perfectly functional, aimed a withering attack upon the Scottish artillery, rendering it useless, and continued to decimate the Scottish forces. In the disarray two sections of James's army left the hilltop, without orders, and swept down toward the English lines, coming down with such force that they at first broke through the English ranks. Blasted by accurate artillery fire and seeing what he took to be a sign of victory in this unplanned charge, James led his remaining forces down the hill in a massive sweep toward the enemy.

The early Scottish attacks were soon engulfed by the English and James's massive horde fell upon the merciless bills, expertly brandished by Howard's troops, which sliced the spiked heads from the simple pikes of the Scots infantry. Unable now to fight at close enough range, the Scots were massacred in vast numbers with James himself falling, within yards of Howard, sword in hand.

The weaponry, the bridge, and the charge… all big mistakes.

ABOVE: A Flodden memorial.

BELOW: King James IV.

The Battle of Saratoga

The American War of Independence from 1775 came about initially as a result of discontent amongst the American colonists with the taxes imposed upon them by the distant English government. Famously this led to the Boston Tea Party, where fervent protesting settlers tipped shiploads of valuable tea into the ocean. The English response to this, and other revolutionary acts, was to impose military rule that, after spirited resistance, led inexorably to war.

■ **ABOVE: General John Burgoyne.**

In 1777 the charismatic commander of the English force entrusted with the task of taking control of Lake Champlain, and ultimately the entire Hudson River valley, was one General John Burgoyne, who was, at various times, a soldier, playwright, politician, and celebrated party animal. Well connected – and not short of self-confidence – he was known affectionately by his men as Gentleman Johnny.

He had personally convinced his superiors in London of the wisdom of his plan, which was to drive south from the lake with the intention of meeting another English force, led by Sir William Howe, moving north from New York State. This would, in his estimation, split New England from the other states and generally demoralize the American revolutionaries. However, it did not quite work out that way.

As Burgoyne took his forces

southward he boasted publicly about his ability to call upon the help of Native American Indians in his military endeavor – even sending out a written notice to his troops – stating that "thousands" were at his beck and call. This statement, which ultimately proved to be inaccurate, riled the Americans – especially as a terrible incident took place at the end of July 1777 that enraged them further. Although afterward disputed, the news spread like wildfire that a beautiful young woman, Jane McCrea, who was following her fiancée in Burgoyne's army, had been taken and brutally scalped by native savages. This atrocity fired an even more determined resolve in the Americans to defy their British "masters" and throw off the cloak of imperialist rule.

Burgoyne's campaign began with some success. Moving south toward his first objective, Fort Ticonderoga on Lake Champlain in northern New York State, the American force there anticipated the strength of his attack and retreated afloat with their artillery and supplies. Burgoyne pursued them down to Hubbardton, where he engaged them in battle and came away victorious. This was a good start, but as he contemplated moving south toward Albany with his 7,000 English and German troops, dark clouds began to gather. He expected to meet Sir William Howe's troops at his next destination but now learned that Howe was engaged elsewhere – in a fight for Philadelphia – and would not make the rendezvous. He also began to understand that he could not, in fact, rely upon support from Native Americans and, at the same time, his lines of supply from Canada were becoming less and less robust.

It was now that Burgoyne was faced with a crucial decision. Should he, as both options were available to him, move south by water or land? He elected to march south overland, and this was a major blunder.

ABOVE: The battlefield of the Battle of Saratoga, now part of Saratoga National Historic Park, in Stillwater, New York.

BELOW: Major General Philip John Schuyler.

The American commander, Major General Philip Schuyler, who, despite the fact that he was not actually present, was desperate to restore his reputation after the uncontested loss of Fort Ticonderoga, realized that he now had an opportunity to weaken the English forces by employing a "scorched earth" policy in front of the advancing army. Destroying roads and bridges, creating small landslides, felling trees, and redirecting streams and rivers, Schuyler turned Burgoyne's progress south into a nightmare. In addition, he destroyed crops and removed livestock, so that the English became under-resourced and even more reliant upon their failing lines of supply. Burgoyne could only progress at the rate of one mile per day and the constant repair of bridges and the clearing of roads exhausted his army.

Suffering from lack of supplies, Burgoyne sent off a column of his troops to attack a well-stocked supply base at Bennington, expecting an easy victory. He miscalculated. Led

by General John Stark, the New Hampshire militia scored a crushing victory in the ensuing battle, resulting in the deaths of over 200 English soldiers and the capture of a further 700, while suffering only 80 killed and wounded.

Working hard politically behind the scenes, Schuyler was amassing an army of increasing size to finally face the British advance, now weakened by losses, delays, exhaustion, and shortages, and was successful in this – but was relieved of his command before the last act was played out. However, Burgoyne's force was now seriously depleted and thrown back upon its own meager resources.

The opposing armies eventually met at the first Saratoga battle at Freeman's Farm on September 19, where the English won only a pyrrhic victory, losing over 600 men to the rebels' 400. With hundreds of wounded and exhausted troops, without further support and with no supplies, Burgoyne's army was now in a desperate state.

When the final battle of Saratoga came, on October 7, the blunders had all been made and the English were already defeated. Their failure to plan and communicate effectively, their over-optimistic view of help from Native Americans, their decision to travel by land rather than by water, and their inability to maintain sufficient supplies brought them to a defeat of staggering proportions. They were down to less than 6,500 men and they faced an American force of over 7,000 led by the American General Gates. Burgoyne was the aggressor and launched his attack, but his men were driven back and the action ended in retreat. Finally what remained of his army was surrounded by superior forces and, 10 days later, nearly 6,000 English and German troops surrendered to the Americans. Burgoyne had lost 86% of his original army.

This victory over the British was of such magnitude that it convinced France to enter the war as an ally of America, and would ultimately lead to American independence.

■ **ABOVE: A depiction of American riflemen from Colonel Daniel Morgan's Provisional Rifle Corps at the Battle of Saratoga, October 7, 1777.**

■ **LEFT: The scene of the surrender of the British General John Burgoyne at Saratoga, October, 1777.**

The Battle of Bladensburg

When, during the War of 1812, the British engineered an opportunity to attack Washington, the US high command was unconvinced that it would ever happen. And they suffered from another serious problem… they had too many leaders!

As English forces moved toward Bladensburg, and because of its proximity to the capital, the commander of the American forces, Brigadier General William Winder, met not only with many members of the Cabinet, but also the President, James Madison, to discuss the military position. Indeed, many of them, including the Secretary of

State James Monroe, decamped to Bladensburg to personally oversee the operation. The result has been called "the greatest disgrace ever dealt to American arms."

A war had been declared upon the British Empire by America in 1812 but, for the first two years, not many people came. The British had been pre-occupied with Napoleon in Europe and had not been able to send significant forces to the US, but by 1814 Napoleon was defeated and exiled and finally the British could turn their attention to the Americans, who had numerous grievances and potential ambitions in Canada.

For two years the opposing navies had achieved an edgy standoff with the British – under the command of the brilliant Alexander Cochrane (years later to be remembered as the fictional Horatio Hornblower) – having control of Chesapeake Bay. Now a large army of veterans, led by Major General Robert Ross, was on its way to link up with Cochrane's already considerable force. This presented the opportunity to the British, under the overall command of the Governor General of Canada, Lieutenant General Sir George Prevost, to launch a complex series of attacks and diversions upon the American enemy. Prevost would lead his troops down into America and invade New York State while later, from the south, Cochrane would split his ship-based forces from his powerful position in Chesapeake Bay and threaten both Baltimore and Washington.

The Americans had a naval presence in Chesapeake Bay in the form of a flotilla commanded by Commodore Joshua Barney. Cochrane sent a small number of vessels up the Potomac River toward Alexandria in a maneuver against Washington, while advancing with his main force into the Patuxent to push back the American ships. So successful was this move that Barney was forced to scuttle his own ships on August 22 and retreat on foot toward the capital. Meanwhile

ABOVE: A statue of President James Madison located at the Library of Congress James Madison Memorial Building.

LEFT: The burning of Washington.

Ross, now without the American navy to contend with, had landed his men and was proceeding inland along the river to reach Upper Marlboro where he paused to regroup and decide upon his next course of action – attack Washington or Baltimore? He chose Washington.

The commander of the area around Washington was Brigadier General William Winder – a man with limited military experience. His command, on paper, numbered over 15,000 men but in reality was much smaller than that, and poorly trained. Nonetheless, he moved his men forward, crossing the Eastern Branch of the Potomac to meet Ross at Upper Marlboro, where he came off worst on August 22 and retreated immediately.

Winder had already ordered the force under the command of Brigadier General Stansbury to move from Baltimore to defend Bladensburg, as he reasoned that this was a crucial axis point in the defense of Washington, and Stansbury now held a commanding position above the town. But when he heard of Winder's retreat back across the river – and of his intention to burn the bridge – Stansbury panicked and led his men away from his well-defended location, leaving Bladensburg behind, and crossed the Bladensburg Bridge which, unfortunately, he forgot to burn in his hurry to find safety.

Stansbury now positioned his forces poorly, in particular his field artillery, which did not have a sufficient field of fire to hold the unburnt bridge from capture. At this crucial moment Winder appeared on the scene with the politician James Monroe, who began rearranging the American forces at will while Winder moved three regiments into positions even more exposed to British fire.

By now Stansbury was supported by a further force, led by Brigadier General Walter Smith, to his rear and right, but due to poor

■ ABOVE: **Alexander Cochrane.**

■ BELOW: **Brigadier General William Winder.**

communication, there was a gap a mile wide between their two positions. At the same time, Joshua Barney's men brought a number of naval guns to the fight. Most of the American men, either through constant reorganization or forced marches, were extremely tired.

Around midday on August 24, Ross arrived at the undefended Bladensburg, the American forces now positioned across the river that still had a crossable bridge. An English advance, led by Colonel William Thornton, was at first repelled but since the American guns only shot ball, rather than the grape or chain best suited to such an encounter, they eventually made the crossing. Simultaneously, another English force had forded the river above the town. Winder counter-attacked but, partly due to his own confusing orders and partly due to the vicious English Congreve rockets, his troops were scattered.

Both Smith and Barney fought on, with Barney's naval men and guns inflicting serious damage to the British advance, but eventually even they could not hold the British onslaught, and Winder ordered a retreat. Sadly his muddled order did not reach Barney, who fought on while the rest of the American forces left the field of battle. In the end, finally overcome and personally badly wounded, Barney also summoned his men to retreat.

In the final moments of the inevitable retreat, the ineffectual Winder issued confusing and contradictory instructions about where his fleeing troops should go or how they should reform and, in the end, they mostly left the area in panic.

For all of the ferocity of the engagement, during which nearly 7,000 Americans faced approximately 4,500 British, the losses were relatively slight. The British killed numbered 64 along with 185 wounded. The American army, which had turned and run so quickly, lost only around 50 men killed and 100 captured.

The encounter is notable for the dismal failure of American strategy and leadership and the collapse of their resolve in battle.

The British, after a rest in the summer heat, took Washington later that same day.

Leadership

Napoleon commented, "I have plenty of clever generals but just give me a lucky one." In war, as in so many other spheres of life, it is the quality of leadership that is paramount. Over the course of history some generals have been inspirational, others have been successful, but many have been disastrous. This is equally true of many of the politicians behind them. The history of World War II was dominated by a number of political leaders – most obviously Hitler and Stalin – whose limited military prowess was more than matched by an overarching belief in their own ability.

Hitler, who had reached the high rank of corporal in the German army during World War I, was ruthless in his control over the military high command, often placing unrealistic demands upon his generals – such as the instruction to General Paulus not to withdraw from Stalingrad in 1942 that resulted in a major defeat when the German army was trapped by the Russian counter-attack in a classic pincer movement – while encouraging unproductive disputes amongst them. Toward the end of the war, Hitler, embattled within his bunker in Berlin, issued instructions to armies that had long ceased to be in the forlorn hope that the tide of war could be reversed.

Stalin too had demonstrated a ruthlessness of command when, during the 1930s, he had purged many of the higher echelons of the Russian military command with the result that, when faced by the German invasion of June 1941, his army lacked the experienced commanders capable of swiftly launching a counter-offensive.

Even relatively successful generals had their failings. Lieutenant General Mark W. Clark's actions in Italy, following the protracted landings at Salerno, demonstrated an almost obsessional thirst for personal glory. So determined was he that his force should liberate Rome – a feat achieved in June 1944 – that he ignored a weakness in the German lines, allowing the bulk of the German army to escape northward to reinforce the Gothic Line and prolong the military campaign in Italy.

■ RIGHT: **Napoleon Bonaparte.**

■ BELOW: **Adolf Hitler.**

The Battle of New Orleans

Just five months after their disaster at Bladensburg and the loss of Washington, the Americans had their revenge in a great victory over the British in the battle for New Orleans – even though, when it was fought, the war had already ended.

The great General Andrew Jackson foresaw the potential British assault on New Orleans and arrived in the city on December 1, 1814 to find a city completely unprepared for an attack. He immediately set about building defenses and summoning an army of militia to withstand the oncoming British assault. He ultimately assembled a force of 6,000 men, comprising many seasoned marksmen from several Southern states.

Just a few weeks later the British arrived by sea in the Gulf of Mexico. Unknown to their commander, Sir Edward Pakenham, a peace treaty was about to be signed on December 24 but he had been at sea with his men and the news had not reached him. With his force of 7,500 soldiers on board he quickly overcame the American naval defenses and soon landed his men on the banks of the Mississippi some eight miles from New Orleans.

On the night of December 23, just one day before peace was distantly declared, the Americans launched an attack, which was repulsed, but at a loss to the British of 400 men. Jackson then quickly withdrew his forces to their carefully prepared positions behind their entrenched defenses.

Here was the first British blunder… they had no intelligence about the American defenses to inform their attack and they knew little about the terrain.

The land between the British army and New Orleans was boggy and difficult but they advanced without further impediment from the enemy. However, when Pakenham's force of 7,000 men came within sight of their American foe they began to understand the clever obstacles that Jackson had laid out for them.

ABOVE: The Battle of New Orleans, painted by Edward Percy Moran.

To their left was the Mississippi River, where a ship and several gunboats were stationed, and at a turning in the road were several houses, concealing American troops. To their right was a heavy swamp, bordered by a road fortified with powerful batteries. In front of them was a canal, behind which Jackson had thrown up impressive breastworks from where his expert marksmen could

pick off the advancing troops.

Almost as soon as the head of the British column arrived upon the central ground, heavy and devastating fire opened from left, right, and center. The American artillery rained

■ **RIGHT: General Andrew Jackson.**

■ **ABOVE: A bird's-eye view of the Battle of New Orleans, January 8, 1815.**

destruction upon the British column while the marksmen behind the fortifications proved their worth in deadly accurate fire. To add to the carnage, Jackson had filled the houses to the left with explosives and, at the opportune moment, his men fired upon the houses, which were blasted apart with terrible force, killing and maiming the British over a great area nearby. After much loss, the British were forced to withdraw and set up camp outside of the range of the American guns.

As yet undaunted, over several days Pakenham brought up heavier batteries and placed them, in the dead of night, to surprise his enemy. On the misty morning of January 1, 1815 he opened fire and initially confused the Americans. Had the British charged at this point they might have gained a surprise victory… but they did not and the Americans rallied, eventually forcing the British from the field once again.

Now a further ambitious plan from Pakenham involved the digging of a new canal to advance boats with artillery, men, and supplies. The work was completed by January 6 but failed as the banks of the new waterway caved in, leaving only room for small boats to pass through.

Pakenham intended to attack on January 8 with 1,400 additional men approaching from his new canal. Due to the obstacles only 300 men made it through, and they were late. At the same time the ladders and other necessary equipment to bridge the canal and overcome the breastworks did not appear on time. The British attacked without the benefit of a bombardment from the heavy guns that had not made it down the canal and, ultimately, they were repulsed.

Pakenham, who was always present and at the head of his troops, was killed and the British lost 2,000 men killed or wounded. The American losses numbered only eight killed and 13 wounded.

The battle was a massive victory for the Americans and their national pride swelled as a result. But it was all unnecessary, as the war was already over. This was the last time that Britain and America would face each other in battle.

The Retreat from Kabul

ABOVE: **Major General William Elphinstone.**

Although still in the general area of "underestimating the enemy," there is a particularly devastating blunder that has occasionally been made by commanders who have been completely taken in, and deceived, by their opponent. History proves that it is a mistake to trust the word of an enemy. Rarely has this failure to be resolute in the face of threat been so clear – and so costly – as in the dealings between Major General William Elphinstone and Amir Akbar Khan in the Afghanistan city of Kabul. The result was a massacre that defies comparison.

The British had occupied Kabul in 1839 and suppressed the local Afghan population, setting up a cozy Victorian lifestyle for the political and officer classes. They had a force of 4,500 men under their command, plus over 12,000 civilian workers, families, and camp followers within their protection.

The Afghans hated the domination of this arrogant foreign power and seethed for revenge, establishing an aggressive resistance movement led by the ambitious Prince Akbar Khan. Meanwhile, the complacent British put in place a new and weak commander, Elphinstone, who was by now over 60 years old and already had a reputation as an incompetent fool. The British political agent, William Macnaghten, assisted him.

Sensing weakness, Akbar Khan and the local forces increased their aggression and, following an uprising on November 2, 1841, they attacked and murdered a senior diplomat, Sir Alexander Burnes, in his own home within the city. Elphinstone did nothing. Soon after this Akbar Khan took up a position above the British troops, now poorly sited outside of the main Kabul citadel, and bombarded their position. Elphinstone eventually sent out a force to dislodge them but this was repulsed with the loss of 300 men dead and wounded.

Now under constant attack and harassment, and with growing casualties, the ageing and sick Elphinstone took no further action, ignoring the pleas from his officers, while Macnaghten tried to negotiate a retreat with the enemy. Akbar Khan called Macnaghten to a meeting but killed him and his entourage as soon as they arrived, later dragging the agent's body through the streets of the city.

Weakened, surrounded, and with morale falling apart, the British General was frozen in the headlights of Afghan aggression. Ultimately, despite Akbar Khan's previous treachery, Elphinstone signed an agreement of surrender which guaranteed him a safe withdrawal for his troops and followers – over 16,000 people – to Jalalabad, about 90 miles away. The agreement had the additional promise from Akbar Khan of an escort and supplies for the journey for which, in return, he agreed to surrender his arms and leave his sick and wounded behind.

His officers wanted him to stay and defend Kabul but Elphinstone was intent upon retreat. He had trusted the word of Akbar… but Akbar Khan had lied.

On the morning of January 6, 1842, the huge column of troops, workers, civilians, women, and children moved slowly out of Kabul, safe in the knowledge that they would be protected on their journey and that those that had been left behind would be looked after. However, as soon as they had left the area, the Afghans swooped down and began firing at their rear while others entered the city and began killing the remaining residents and torching the town.

By the next day it was clear that all was not well. There was no escort, there was no safe passage, and there were no supplies. Once again Elphinstone met with Akbar

ABOVE: **Prince Akbar Khan.**

Khan and, convinced once again by his lies, agreed to delay his retreat and also hand over several hostages. As a result, he slowed their progress. Meanwhile Akbar Khan was positioning his army along the path to Jalalabad.

Elphinstone's blunder now was fully exposed. The agreements that he had made were worthless. Once again his officers implored him to turn back to Kabul but Elphinstone would have none of it. They were now bound for Jalalabad and their fate was sealed.

Moving slowly forward, the column was picked off by the Afghans at will. At one point several hundred soldiers deserted, only to be captured and killed by the enemy. By now Elphinstone was no longer capable of giving any orders. Some of the wives and children were promised safety and left the decimated column, only to be killed later. Even now Elphinstone and his second in command were persuaded to become hostages in defense of the remaining

BELOW: Remnants of an Army, by Elizabeth Butler, portraying William Brydon arriving at the gates of Jalalabad.

column. They both died later.

The slaughter continued. Slowly, defenseless thousands, including women and children, were annihilated and on January 13 – just eight days from when they had set out – one single British officer arrived at Jalalabad on horseback.

He had a severe head wound and his horse was wounded. The horse lay down in a stable and never recovered. When asked what had happened to the army, the officer, William Brydon, replied "I am the army."

RIGHT: Sir Alexander Burnes.

The Charge of the Light Brigade

As General the Lord Fitzroy James Henry Somerset Raglan, the 66-year-old commander of the British troops in Crimea, stood and surveyed the scene spread out before him on a cold October morning in 1854, he could feel quite satisfied with his return to combat duty after a gap of well over 30 years. His illustrious active military career, largely spent at the side of Wellington as his military secretary, had ended at Waterloo, where a wound to his arm had led to amputation. A succession of the highest ranking diplomatic posts had followed but it was Russia's expansionist activities in the last few years that had finally brought him to the Crimea, accompanied in this endeavor by a suitably aristocratic set of staff and officers, with a plan to destroy the Russian's fleet at Sebastopol and put a halt to their Mediterranean ambitions. Soon after their landing at the Black Sea port of Calamita Bay, his forces, alongside his French allies, had encountered the Russians at the river of Alma and had won a notable victory against a well-defended force. Indeed, he felt that he had even achieved a certain personal victory by securing an important position on a high ridge on Telegraph

Hill, overlooking the battle, with only his staff in tow – despite the fact that some had claimed that he had stumbled there by mistake.

Raglan liked to be on high ridges and, from his current raised vantage point on the Sapoune Ridge, the northern-most of two valleys swept out before him, rising on his left to form the Fedioukine Hills. At his end of the broad valley plain his Light Brigade was reforming after several skirmishes, their bright reds and metals glinting in the morning sun. Away to his right a further escarpment formed the other valley side, the Woronzov Heights then sweeping down to the right into the south valley beyond, to where his Heavy Brigade had repulsed the Russians earlier in the morning. Away in front, toward the end of the north valley, the Russians had secured a strong position defended by numerous heavy guns, their forces spreading out along both hillsides toward the British position, forming what would become the "valley of death."

While it may have occurred to Raglan that this northern deployment would require careful management, at this moment his attention was drawn to activity in the south valley where a small contingent of Russian artillery men were removing some of the allied guns abandoned in the earlier encounters. He was well aware that such gains were often used as confirmation of victory and, to him, this Russian affront was unacceptable. He decided to send in his Light Cavalry – the perfect weapon against such a small force.

The cavalry was under the command of the arrogant Lieutenant General Lucan and beneath him the Light Brigade was led by his estranged brother-in-law Major General the Earl of Cardigan. There was no love lost between the two.

Raglan, wanting to regain the territory to his right, had already that morning issued an order to Lucan stating "Cavalry to advance and take advantage of any opportunity to recover the heights. They will be supported by the infantry which have been ordered to advance on two fronts." But little action had followed. This may have been due to a confusion

"They swept proudly past, glittering in the morning sun in all the pride and splendour of war. We could hardly believe the evidence of our senses! Surely that handful of men were not going to charge an army in position?"

William Howard Russell – Times correspondent

■ ABOVE: **An archive photo of the 8th Hussars.**

caused by the vague geographical reference of the message or possibly by the acidic relationship between Lucan and Cardigan who were known to be at each other's throats. Perhaps in frustration, Raglan fired off a further order specifically to stop the Russians removing the guns in the south valley – "Lord Raglan wishes the cavalry to advance rapidly to the front, follow the enemy and try to prevent the enemy carrying away the guns. Troop horse artillery may accompany. French cavalry is on your left. Immediate."

The order was written on his behalf by Brigadier Airey and sent for dispatch by the young Captain Nolan who galloped down to where Lucan was positioned, about 600 feet below Raglan's viewpoint. From his lower position Lucan could not see into the valley on his right and had no view of the Russians pulling away the captured guns. Bemused by the wording Lucan asked what guns he should attack. Nolan, full of self-importance, gestured with a vague sweep of his arm and declared, "There my Lord is your enemy… there are your guns." Feeling it beneath him to question Nolan further, Lucan assumed that the order meant that he must attack the Russian emplacement before him at the far end of the north valley and accordingly cantered down to pass the order on to Cardigan.

The blunder had occurred. As a result, beneath the morning sunshine of that October morning, Cardigan led his 673 cavalrymen down the north valley, toward the heavily defended Russian position less than one mile away.

With Cardigan at their front and setting off at a trot, the Light Brigade advanced, despite having no infantry support, toward the enemy's artillery. Nolan, perhaps realizing that a terrible error had been made, pursued the column and galloped frantically in front of Cardigan waving wildly. But at that moment a shell burst nearby and Nolan fell, becoming the first man to die in the charge. Moments later the first line was within range of the Russian guns which opened fire, blasting great holes in the British forces and, exposed as they were to enemy attack from both sides of the valley, the Light's men and horses were decimated by hostile fire.

While terrible damage was done the cavalry did eventually break through the Russian line and momentarily scattered the enemy troops behind. However, still under fire from both sides of the valley, the remainder of the Light Brigade had to turn and try to escape to their own lines.

Cardigan reached the guns and broke through the Russian lines. He then turned and, without rallying his troops or organizing their retreat, made his own way back to safety. He later dined on his yacht in Balaclava Harbor. Lucan, who was meant to follow up the Light's attack with his Heavy Brigade, turned back after seeing the carnage.

Of those that eventually returned only 195 were still mounted, while 118 men had been killed, with 127 wounded, and 60 taken as prisoner. Some 335 horses perished in the confrontation. The entire action had taken less than 25 minutes.

Cardigan eventually returned home to a hero's welcome. Lucan, much criticized, defended himself in a speech in the House of Lords and was finally appointed Knight Commander of the British Empire in 1855.

Lord Raglan died of natural causes before the end of the Crimean conflict.

■ BELOW: **Captain Louis Nolan.**

Strategy

Before engaging in any military action it was, and remains, essential to have a coherent strategy. This strategy might be developed over a long period of time in the face of real or perceived threats or it could be thrown together at the last minute in order to deal with an immediate crisis, as occurred in 1982 when Britain rapidly put together a naval task force to recapture the Falkland Islands following the Argentinean invasion. The fact that the invasion occurred in the first place was, however, a failure of earlier British strategic thinking when it was announced the previous year that the country's military presence in the South Atlantic was to be reduced, thereby suggesting to the Argentinean military junta that Britain would be unwilling or unable to defend the islands.

Fifty years earlier, Britain's empire was at its peak but the threats that the empire faced were increasing. Central to the empire was India and the other colonies in the Far East. Two rival powers – Japan and the USA – started to emerge in the early years of the 20th century and both potentially threatened British power in the Pacific. In the years prior to World War II Britain developed a defensive strategy for its imperial possessions based upon the island of Singapore. A huge naval dockyard was constructed on the island along with a chain of supply bases linking it to Britain. Unfortunately, British strategists had failed to ensure sufficient soldiers, tanks, and aircraft to the defense of Malaya and Singapore and, with the Japanese attacks following Pearl Harbor in December 1941, Malaya and Singapore quickly surrendered. Of the 140,000 British and Empire troops defending Singapore, 130,000 surrendered; Churchill described the defeat as "the worst disaster and largest capitulation in British history."

Equally disastrous can be the changing of a strategy halfway through a campaign. During the summer of 1940, the German air force, the Luftwaffe, sought to gain air superiority during the Battle of Britain by attacking the Royal Air Force's airfields; this tactic had the result of fundamentally weakening the RAF's ability to fight back. However, just at the point that victory might be achieved, the Luftwaffe switched its attention to bombing London – the start of the Blitz – with the result that the RAF was able to regroup and ultimately win the battle.

BELOW: An Argentinian bomb explodes on board the Royal Navy frigate HMS *Antelope* killing the bomb disposal engineer who was trying to defuse it. The ship was part of the British task force engaged in the recapture of the Falkland Islands.

The Battle of Antietam

ABOVE: Allan Pinkerton, President Abraham Lincoln, and Major General John A. McClernand. This photo was taken not long after the Civil War's first battle on northern soil in Antietam, Maryland on October 3, 1862.

BELOW: Artillery Hell – early morning looking north along the Hagerstown Turnpike.

Looking back, it is hard to review the active Civil War military career of George Brinton McClellan with much sympathy. Clearly a successful planner and a great organizer he was, history indicates, better behind a desk than in front of one. President Lincoln himself damned McClellan with faint praise when he recorded "If he can't

fight himself, he excels in making others ready to fight."

Sun Tzu in his *Art of War*, written in 500BC, noted five dangerous faults that can lead a commander to defeat. One of them was cowardice and another was "over-solicitude for his men." Perhaps the latter best describes McClellan's actions at Antietam – and indeed he was certainly very popular with his troops. However, on the field, and faced with an aggressive enemy, he tended to falter, frequently over-estimating the size of the opposing forces, and often retreating to save his troops from a fight. He also liked to set up his headquarters well to the rear of the battle… so much so that he was technically absent during many encounters.

During the earlier Peninsula Campaign he had retreated more than once before Robert E. Lee's smaller army, causing Lincoln to pen the withering request:

ABOVE: The Battle of Antietam, 1862; Confederate dead at Bloody Lane, looking northeast from the south bank.

"My dear McClellan: If you don't want to use the army, I would like to borrow it for a while. Yours respectfully, A. Lincoln."

The President was not a fan.

At Antietam, where once again he faced his old nemesis Lee, McClellan brought all of these traits into play. Encamped well behind the field of battle, McClellan was commanding his 75,000 men by remote control. Lee had only 38,000 men, but McClellan was convinced that the Confederate army was far larger – and failed to update his information with adequate cavalry reconnaissance.

At first light, on September 17, an attack was launched upon Lee's left flank that met with strong defiance from the Confederate forces. This was the first of many attacks and counters that raged back and forth with huge losses on both sides. McClellan's men finally broke through the Confederate line but this brief victory was not backed up with adequate strength and the advantage was lost as quickly as it had been achieved. Later the Union forces captured a bridge across Antietam Creek and were now in a position to attack Lee's right flank, but the timely arrival of Confederate reinforcements once again cancelled out their brief advantage.

At no time did McClellan's men concentrate enough force to completely overwhelm the enemy – even though they were vastly superior in numbers. Lee was throwing his entire force into the desperate battle, but the cautious McClellan was holding vast numbers in reserve. It was later estimated that his reserve force was greater than the entire Confederate army.

The fierce fighting raged throughout the day with massive losses on both sides – 12,400 men killed and wounded from the Union, and over 10,300 Confederates. With 23,000 casualties, this was the bloodiest single day battle of the war.

During the night Lee withdrew his forces, while maintaining sporadic attacks against the Union troops. Technically, he had lost the battle but McClellan had failed to crush his army from a position that could have ended the war. Even worse, McClellan chose not to pursue the weakened Lee's retreat, allowing him to reform and fight another day.

Although the victory at Antietam was politically very useful to the Union cause, Lincoln soon removed McClellan from active command.

The Battle of Little Bighorn

For such a famous and well-documented encounter, there remains much mystery and divided opinion about the Battle of Little Bighorn, as indeed there does about the US Commander on the field, General George Custer. To millions he became a flamboyant tragic hero, but to many who served under him he was arrogant and vain. To those above him, he was troublesome and insubordinate. However, nobody ever doubted his bravery, and the man – as well as his spectacular defeat – has passed into American folklore.

In 1876 the plight of the North American Plains Indians was becoming desperate. Over the preceding years they had been corralled into settlement areas – or reservations – removing their ancient right to the freedom of the plains. Even worse, the white Americans had broken treaty after treaty with the Indian tribes, constantly moving the boundaries and reducing the prescribed enclosures in order to free up areas where they could lay claim to large gold deposits. Whenever the Indians resisted the American restrictions they were identified as "hostile." The Indians were trying to protect their homeland… and the white Americans were trying to steal it.

The commanding rule of the whites led the resisting natives to unite in self defense, and by May 1876, a force of 10,000 tribesmen – consisting of forces from the Cheyenne, Sioux, Lakota, and Arapaho – came together on the banks of the Little Bighorn River in Montana.

Amongst others, General Alfred Terry was given the job of finding and controlling this native resistance. He put Custer in charge of the 7th Cavalry with an instruction to locate and help encircle the Indian fighters. Poor intelligence meant that nobody on the American side of this conflict ever understood the size of the army against them and Custer rode against a force of unimaginable size.

And so it happened that on June 24, 1876, Custer, with his troop of 600 men, halted close to the Little Bighorn River and sent out his scouts to locate the native enemy. Custer had already been offered extra men and Gatlin guns by Terry, but he had refused them, confident that the 7th could easily overcome a bunch of Plains Indians. Instructed by Terry to await reinforcements in order to encircle the gathering native force, Custer wanted to go for glory and make a surprise direct attack upon the enemy encampment, which, unknown to him, was almost three miles long. However, the element of surprise was lost as he had to cross a nearby creek during the hours of daylight and was spotted by a group of Indians.

Although warned of the size of the encampment, from Custer's viewpoint he could only see women and children, or boys feeding horses. He assumed that any warriors were asleep.

Deciding now to attack, without further delay, Custer split his troop into four sections, giving command of three to Major Reno, Captain Benteen, and Captain McDougall, who would escort the pack train. Benteen was sent off to reconnoiter the area while Reno took up an attacking position further south in hills above the Little Bighorn River. At 3pm on June 25 Reno crossed the river and immediately fell under heavy and unexpected resistance from a well-prepared and determined enemy. After fierce fighting, Reno was forced to pull back across the river, losing more men in the retreat. At the same time Benteen had received direct orders from Custer to return to give support and, with McDougall and the pack train in tow, he met up with Reno in his original position in the hills, where they dug in against the

ABOVE: General George Custer with his wife Elizabeth.

OPPOSITE: Dull Knife (Tah-me-la-pash-me), Chief of the Northern Cheyennes, at the Battle of Little Bighorn.

advancing Indian forces. Custer was now isolated.

Even though he could hear distinct volley fire from Custer's position – a clear sign of the need for support – Benteen stayed with Reno's troops, where they continued the fight until reinforcements arrived two days later. Meanwhile a massive force of Indians crossed the river to the north and attacked Custer and his 200 men. It is thought that as many as 3,000 Native Americans attacked.

Custer, and every one of his men and horses, was killed within an hour, and, as there were no army survivors from the "Last Stand," exactly what happened is still a matter of some conjecture. By the time Terry arrived with reinforcements on June 27, most of the dead soldiers had been stripped and mutilated. Custer's body only had two bullet wounds.

Although there were many individual acts of great courage and bravery, the tragedy of Little Bighorn seems to have been the result of a lack of discipline alongside a massive failure of intelligence. Had Custer waited for General Terry to arrive the massacre could have been avoided.

LEFT: The Custer Fight, by Charles Marion Russell. It shows the Battle of Little Bighorn, from the Indian side.

BELOW: An iron sculpture, by native artist Colleen Cutschall, honoring the Native Americans. It was placed next to the old memorial for General Custer.

The Battle of Isandlwana

ABOVE: The Isandlwana Hills in Kwazulu-Natal. The rockpile in the foreground is one of many marking the location of British mass graves at the site.

Perhaps the starkest example of the error of under-estimating the enemy happened at Isandlwana on January 22, 1879.

The British, a Victorian imperialist power who already controlled the colony of Natal in southeast Africa, viewed their neighbors in Zululand across the River Tugela with suspicion and saw this savage people as a threat. Using an incident in December 1878, where a number of Zulus were accused of murdering some British subjects, the British launched an attack, secure in the belief that their highly trained force, well armed with modern weaponry, would easily overcome the local tribesmen armed only with short spears and hide shields. They were wrong.

On January 11, 1879, the British commander-in-chief, Lord Chelmsford, crossed the Tugela into Zululand at Rorke's Drift, leaving a small company of the 24th Foot there to form an advanced base. His first objective was to move into Zulu territory as far as the Isandlwana Hills, some 10 miles from the river border, and from there seek out his enemy in order to engage in battle.

Chelmsford started out with a mixed force of some 15,000 English and Welsh troops, Natal Native Infantry, mounted volunteers, and Natal police. He amended his original plan to split this force into five divisions and opted for only three, one moving toward north Zululand, another moving south to the Indian Ocean coast, and the third – the center column of 4,700 men – marching to Isandlwana, under his direct command. A further force of 1,500, led by Colonel Anthony Durnford, originally intended to be the second column, was available as a back-up to the center, giving that central drive a total of some 6,200 men.

When, after slow progress due to heavy rains and the care of hundreds of pulling oxen, Chelmsford finally reached the lower slopes of the Isandlwana Hills he failed to entrench properly his force. Standing orders dictated that he should form a circle of wagons to form a defensive stronghold… but he did not bother. He thought it would take a week to form such a defensive position and he thought it unnecessary, preferring to engage with the enemy as soon as possible.

Here we witness the heart of the blunder. The colonial British army had fought hundreds of encounters in distant lands with local natives and had always triumphed. Chelmsford – indeed all of the British officers – simply did not understand the numbers, skills, and aggression of the Zulus, assuming easy victories over an untrained rabble of savages. They could not have been more mistaken.

Splitting the force at Isandlwana, Chelmsford took close to 4,000 men into the hills to follow some Zulus who had been discovered by his skirmishers leaving 2,200 men, under the command of Lieutenant Colonel Henry Pulleine, to defend the camp. Chelmsford thought that he was pursuing the main Zulu force but, unknown to him, the Zulus had gone around him and were forming up against Pulleine's position. Meanwhile orders had been sent to Durnford to bring up his men and, when he arrived, he quickly decided to advance upon another group of Zulus who had been seen in the surrounding hills. At no time throughout this entire engagement did the British ever understand the formidable force that opposed them.

The great Zulu king, Cetshwayo, had mobilized a massive force of over 24,000 warriors to "… eat up the red soldiers" of the British army. This force he split in two and about 12,000 dedicated Zulu fighters were now moving in on the Isandlwana encampment. Executing their classic "bull's head" strategy, the Zulu forces made an initial attack centrally which would be pulled back, enticing the British to counter and come forward, allowing them to be encircled and outflanked by the Zulu "horns."

With Chelmsford's men out in the hills and Durnford's force outmaneuvered the remaining British force at Isandlwana was now at the mercy of the Zulu warriors. What followed was a story of great courage, determination and, ultimately, annihilation. The British were wiped out.

BELOW: The defence of Rorke's Drift, 1879.

The Gallipoli Campaign

■ BELOW: **Australian troops arrive in Alexandria, en route to the battlefield on the Gallipoli Peninsula, in 1915.**

War is made by politicians, but should be conducted by soldiers. When the politicians not only make the war but also try to direct it there can be problems. Winston Churchill was made First Lord of the Admiralty late in 1911 and proved to be a modernizer. He was also very bold and opinionated.

Britain declared war on Germany on August 4, 1914 and, very soon, entrenched warfare was spreading through France and Belgium. When the Ottoman Empire entered the war on October 31, 1914 Churchill saw the need to crush them early on, while opening another route from which to attack the Germans without the hindrance of trenches. Against the opposition of some of his admirals and other senior military officers he devised a strategy for a naval attack that would break the Turks and create another route toward Germany. Tolerating no opposition, he forced his plan through.

The plan, based upon the historic supremacy of the British navy, sounded simple. A flotilla of Allied ships would force their way through the Dardanelles Straits and, with a major seaborne bombardment, cripple the Turkish defenses and resolve. It did not prove to be so easy.

When the first of Churchill's ships entered the Straits on February 19, 1915 they began a bombardment of the Turkish onshore positions. The attack made little impact. Some days later a second attack was more successful and prompted the full flotilla, on March 1, to enter the

Straits, only to meet with heavy defensive fire, mines, and torpedoes. Two British, and one French, ships were lost and the naval assault had failed.

With so many Allied resources already in the region it now fell to Lord Kitchener to approve a massive shore landing of troops and he placed General Sir Ian Hamilton in command. He had at his disposal not only British and Irish men but also the Australia and New Zealand Army Corps – the Anzacs – and also

■ **ABOVE: A poster of Lord Kitchener from World War I.**

the French Oriental Expeditionary Corps. By the end of the campaign a force of over 450,000 men was to be thrown at the Gallipoli Peninsula. Unfortunately, poor Allied security meant that the Turks were well aware of the plan and had time to prepare.

An initial strike by the 29th Division in the south, at Cape Helles, was to be backed up with a landing by the Anzacs further north. The 29th was intended to drive north while the Anzacs were to cross the peninsula and cut off the Turkish forces from retreat or reinforcement. But Hamilton had a number of problems. Many of his men were undertrained, his information was out of date, and he had too few boats. The planned landings did not go well.

After fierce fighting and heavy losses in the south, the 29th finally began to move north, only to be stopped on April 28 at the village of Krithia, where they were forced to entrench. Meanwhile the Anzacs had landed successfully, but in the wrong place, and with heavy opposition could not advance beyond their beachhead. From these bogged down positions the Allied war now replicated the trench warfare on the Western front that Churchill had so wanted to avoid.

After two more unsuccessful assaults on Krithia, the British finally had to admit that their southern approach had failed and, as a result, Hamilton led his surviving men back to the sea for a new landing north of the Anzac position. Meanwhile, the Australian and New Zealand troops had fended off a massive attack by the Turks, but had gained no new ground from the first day of their assault. Hamilton arrived by sea but was slow in landing his troops and, once again, the Turkish forces were able to pin them down on the beaches.

Heavy fighting, with terrible losses on both sides, continued sporadically for eight months. Hamilton was replaced in October by Lieutenant General Monro who, assessing the grave position of his remaining force, soon recommended a total evacuation. To his credit this, at least, was well managed.

The whole misguided affair cost Churchill his job and reputation – but more importantly it cost the lives of 44,000 Allied men with a further 97,000 wounded or missing. Of these, over 35,000 killed and wounded came from Australia and New Zealand – by far the greatest military casualties in the history of those relatively small nations. Today their loss is still remembered annually on April 25 – Anzac Day.

■ ABOVE: **Australian stretcher bearers attend to casualties.**

■ BELOW: **Australian soldiers march at the Turkish Memorial in Gallipoli, during the Anzac Day ceremonies.**

Supplies

It's a truism of military life that an army marches on its stomach, as Napoleon was quoted as saying, and the provision of food and other equipment is essential to the success of any military action. Throughout history there have been examples of armies that seemed invincible but which were ultimately to be defeated through a lack of food or munitions. Ironically, in 1812, Napoleon forgot his own words when he was forced to retreat from Moscow with his Grand Army. Although the French army had effectively seized Moscow, the Russian "scorched earth" policy ensured that the French ran critically short of supplies and, during the retreat, Russian forces continued to ensure that the French army was unable to obtain further supplies. Although the accurate number of soldiers that invaded Russia is unknown – estimates vary between 400,000 and 700,000 – as is the number that survived – again estimates vary between 10,000 and 70,000 – it is evident that the ragged army that returned west had suffered mightily.

More than a century later another ambitious commander fell into the same trap, having failed to learn properly the lessons of history. In 1941 Adolf Hitler launched his ill-fated invasion of Russia – Operation Barbarossa – and, like Napoleon before him, was to discover that the rapid Russian retreat to the gates of Moscow resulted in over-stretched supply lines at the point that the harsh Russian winter set in. German troops, with inadequate winter clothing, froze to death in their thousands while the Russians, better prepared, planned for a counter attack. Hitler's obsession with defeating Russia was, moreover, to starve other operations of the men and equipment that might have resulted in victory. In North Africa, Rommel's Afrika Korps advanced rapidly toward the Suez Canal in 1942. The loss of the canal would have fundamentally weakened Britain's ability to fight in the Far East and threaten the nation's oil supplies. However, despite constant pleading, Rommel was denied the extra resources that would have aided his advance. The result was the German defeat at the Battle of El-Alamein in October 1942 and, ultimately, the German loss of North Africa or, as Winston Churchill put it after El Alamein, "Now is not the end. It is not even the beginning of the end. But it is, perhaps, the end of the beginning."

BELOW: General Erwin Rommel, commander of the German Afrika Korps, (left), with an unidentified German officer.

The Battle of the Somme

"With God's help, I feel hopeful. The men are in splendid spirits."

General Douglas Haig, June 30, 1916

In retrospect, it seems like a fairly simple lesson to learn. When innocent young men, each weighed down with 70lb of equipment, march slowly through mud and barbed wire toward a hail of machine gun bullets, they tend to die – and die in their thousands. Odd then, perhaps, that General Haig had not learned this by July 2, 1916… as the day before had been the first day of the Battle of the Somme. The battle, which has become a byword for waste and futility in war, lasted for almost five months, but is defined by its first day.

The war with Germany had raged for two years and had become an entrenched war of attrition. Trenches stretched across Europe and the British, uncomfortable with trench warfare, were not playing as big a role as the French thought appropriate. In order to break the deadlock, the French and British jointly planned an offensive along the River Somme, but as the plans were being finalized, the Germans attacked the French city of Verdun, with devastating effect.

LEFT: General Sir Douglas Haig, (left), commander of the British army on the Western Front during World War I, and General Sir Henry Rawlinson.

BELOW: The Somme: The British advance.

OPPOSITE: Men of the Royal Irish Rifles in their support trenches waiting to move into the line at the Somme.

The French poured their resources into the defense of Verdun and the responsibility for the offensive shifted toward Britain.

The opposing forces were stretched along a front of nearly 25 miles. Facing each other across a "no-mans-land" of ploughed earth, mud, and tangled barbed wire were some 750,000 Allied troops – mostly British – and the much smaller force of about 450,000 Germans.

The British had a very specific view of how the battle was to unfold. They had organized the biggest artillery bombardment in history, which they confidently predicted would destroy the German trenches and most of the enemy force. They had also dug tunnels beneath the German lines and set mines to be detonated at the last moment. Once the bombardment stopped the infantry would go "over the top" and advance, with bayonets fitted, to wipe up the last of the opposing troops. Many of the officers were convinced that, as their troops advanced, they would meet with little opposition. That is not how it worked out.

The Germans were already aware of the impending attack and had prepared exceptionally robust trench defenses in advance. They had, in some places, three lines of defensive trenches but, crucially, had dug far

below these into the forgiving chalk to create deep dugouts in which their troops were defended against artillery fire. Some of these were as much as 40ft below ground level. In addition they had laid massive tracts of very thick barbed wire across no-mans-land that would prove resistant to artillery fire.

After seven days of continuous bombardment, and the detonation of some of the mines, the British guns fell silent. Over one and a half million shells had been fired from the Allied lines. The Germans had sat it out and they, and most of the barbed wire, were intact.

When the brave British and French soldiers finally emerged, in wave after wave, proceeding slowly by order in regimented lines, the German troops went back into their trenches and mowed them down with heavy machinegun fire… line after line, row after row, man after man, boy after boy. In just a few hours 60,000 had become casualties of whom nearly 20,000 died. The Germans lost around 10,000 men, killed, wounded, and taken prisoner.

It is difficult, in hindsight, to conclude anything other than that the British strategy should have been reviewed in the light of this terrible sacrifice. But, amazingly, it was not. Indeed, Haig, although not

in command of accurate statistics by the next day, noted that "... the total casualties are estimated at over 40,000 to date. This cannot be considered severe in view of the numbers engaged..."

Perhaps with a little more understanding, General Sir Beauvoir De Lisle made the cryptic comment that the battle had been a great display of valor but that:

"... its assault only failed of success because dead men can advance no further."

And so, nothing changed. The ineffectual bombardments and the suicidal advances continued for a grueling 141 days. In all, over one million men died or were wounded in that short space and time at the Somme.

The Allies succeeded in taking just seven miles of ground.

■ RIGHT: British infantrymen occupy a shallow trench in a ruined landscape before an advance.

■ BELOW: A carrying party of British troops take a batch of duck-boards across marshy ground, during the Battle of the Somme.

Defense of the Philippines

When the Japanese attacked Pearl Harbor on December 7, 1941, an action that was to bring the United States into the war, they planned simultaneous attacks on other US bases in the Pacific in a massive pre-emptive strike. While Pearl Harbor was a surprise, a Japanese attack on the US protectorate of the Philippines had, in fact, been anticipated due to the already strained relationship between the two countries, and a strengthening military presence was already in place under the general leadership of Douglas MacArthur, who had arrived in July 1941.

MacArthur found himself split between two allegiances – one to the President of the United States and the other to the President of the Philippines. To satisfy the US there was a defensive plan (the Orange Plan) to retreat to the jungles of the mountainous Bataan region, but to satisfy the Philippines he would have to protect Manila. MacArthur was unimpressed by the military abilities of the Japanese and had a vision of meeting them in victory on the beaches. He formulated a plan to harass the approaching Japanese flotilla, using the 16 surface ships and 29 submarines available to him, and to attack the weakened survivors as they landed. He calculated that the Japanese would not attack until the weather improved, which gave him until about April 1942, by which time he expected to have a vastly increased force to meet them. Reinforcements were coming, slowly, but it would not be until April that he would have enough to hold off the enemy. He thought that he would have 200,000 men when he needed them.

What he did not know was that a "Europe first" policy had been agreed between the USA and Britain in June, and that his reinforcements would never arrive.

Although he was promised, and expected, this number, MacArthur currently had 107 P-40 fighters and some 35 heavy B-17 bombers in place, along with his standing force. These were joined by the 4th Marine Regiment – recently come from the defense of Shanghai – of 800 men and the promise of a further 700 marines who were already stationed in the Philippines. As a result, apart from the ships, his defenses comprised some

ABOVE: Francis Sayre, US High Commissioner for the Philippines, left, visits with Lieutenant General Douglas MacArthur in 1941 after MacArthur's appointment as commander of the US Army Forces in the Far East to prepare the Philippines for possible Japanese invasion.

■ **ABOVE: After defending the island for nearly a month, American and Filipino soldiers surrender to Japanese invasion troops.**

135,000 men of the US Army Forces Far East military, spread throughout the region, plus approximately 60,000 Philippine troops, most of whom had received very little training, and 150 aircraft. Nevertheless, he abandoned the defensive plan and prepared for his glorious vision, expecting his reinforcements – and the subsequent Japanese attack – to come in the spring. Unfortunately, the Japanese did not co-operate.

In late November the enemy radioed a message to MacArthur warning of imminent hostile action by the Japanese, instructing him to respond immediately following the first act of war. He was to follow the revised "Rainbow Five" plan – which dictated air strikes against enemy installations within range. At this point MacArthur should have realized that he was in no position to defend the islands – and perhaps he did – but his plans did not alter.

On the morning of December 8, 1941 he received the shocking news of the Japanese attack on Pearl Harbor and it seemed, according to witnesses, to throw him into a confused state of indecision and disbelief. The commander of his air forces, Major General Brereton, brought the news and asked for permission to take to the skies and bomb the Japanese airfields in Formosa. MacArthur said no.

Apparently frozen to the spot MacArthur, despite pressure from Washington, hesitated and turned down further requests to send in the bombers. He was determined not to perform the first act of war, but seems to have completely missed the point that the Japanese had already done so in their earlier Hawaiian attack. He eventually ordered reconnaissance flights, but only after the aircraft had been sent up – with no mission – to avoid being destroyed on the ground. Brereton's air force circled over the Philippines without purpose and had to land for refueling before heading toward Formosa. It was now, with the planes on the ground, that the Japanese struck. Almost all of the US aircraft in the Philippines were destroyed.

As it happened, due to poor visibility over the island of Formosa, the Japanese attack on the Philippines had been delayed and, had the US planes been allowed to take advantage, the crushing defeat that was to follow could have been avoided.

Following continued destruction from Japanese air attacks, and a poor performance from the US submarines, the Japanese ground forces began to arrive in waves from December 20, easily overcoming the US and Filipino defenses, weakened by MacArthur's further blunder of using his least experienced troops in the front line.

The Japanese advanced through the islands like an unstoppable fire and, despite many Allied acts of enormous courage, defiance, and durability, MacArthur's failure to revert to the defensive Orange Plan meant that within weeks the Allied forces crumbled, with the final surrender coming on May 6, 1942.

In all, nearly 100,000 Allied troops were taken prisoner, and suffered terribly at Japanese hands. A further 46,000 were lost, killed, or wounded. The Japanese total casualties numbered approximately 22,000.

Well before the final grinding and bloody defeat and subsequent suffering, Douglas MacArthur was flown to safety in Australia and was awarded the Congressional Medal of Honor by the American President.

BELOW: Shortly after word was received that the USA and Japan were at war, many people evacuated Manila. Shown are the many people who rushed to the banks for cash in Manila on March 30, 1942.

Intelligence

In the build-up to the anticipated attack on northern France – D-Day as it became known – the lack of detailed intelligence was to prove critical. The shortest route across the English Channel is that from Dover to Calais and considerable Allied attempts to convince the Germans that this was the route of the intended invasion were made. The southeast of England became a massive military base for British, Empire, and US forces but much of that visible to aerial reconnaissance was fake – inflatable tanks, for example, creating the impression of a massive build-up in the area suitable for quick shipment across to the area around Calais. Known overall as Operation Bodyguard, the Allied subterfuge comprised a number of parts including two main elements: Fortitude North, designed to indicate an imminent attack on Norway, and Fortitude South, which was designed to show a planned invasion of the Pas de Calais area by the fictional 1st US Army Group notionally under the command of General Patton. The lack of German spies on the ground in Britain meant that this and other subterfuges went undiscovered with the result that, when the actual invasion of Normandy was launched on June 6, 1944, the Germans believed that the invasion was a diversion and that the main force would land around Calais. As a result, the German reserves, based in northern France, were held back for a period, thereby allowing the Allied bridgehead in Normandy to be better established. The failure of German intelligence in the build-up to Normandy was crucial in the ultimate Allied success in the west.

BELOW: People operating "The Enigma Machine," which could decrypt secret messages, during World War II.

The Fall of Singapore

There have been opposing views about what lay behind the fall of Singapore, although nobody disputes that it had a lot to do with the Japanese, and a certain amount of mythology has grown up to obscure the events.

One evaluation of the position is that Britain was convinced that the Japanese would launch a naval attack from the Singapore Straits and that, as a result, all of their defenses – including all of their heavy guns – were in the south and irreversibly directed toward the sea. The alternative view is that Churchill's government had anticipated an attack from the adjacent Malay Peninsula, and indeed had planned for it, but had failed to resource adequately the necessary defense.

Either way, it was a major blunder and led to the biggest military surrender in British history and the loss of Britain's most important strategic outpost in Asia. The Allied force of British, Australian, Indian, and local troops numbered some 85,000. The invading Japanese had only 36,000 men.

What is certainly true is that there was an ill-judged air of complacency surrounding the stronghold of Singapore in December 1941, which was thought to be indestructible. Seemingly ignorant of the massive Japanese threat, British life went on as normal with society parties at the Raffles Hotel and officers amusing themselves in the Singapore Club. There was a local view that it was inconceivable that the Japanese would attack through the swamps and jungle of the Peninsula to the north and there was a general underestimation of the Japanese as a fighting force.

This was a common blunder in itself, and was being repeated at exactly the same time at Pearl Harbor and by MacArthur in the Philippines. When the Japanese attack came, in all three places, it was well planned, determined, well executed, ferocious, bloody, and very fast. It all started on December 7, 1941.

The Japanese assault on the Allied

■ **OPPOSITE: Raffles Place, in the heart of the city of Singapore, 1941.**

■ **BELOW: On the shoulders of this quartet will fall the major share of the burden of directing the defense of besieged Singapore. Left to right: Lieutenant General Percival, Major General Sir Ibrahim, Major General Playfair, and Major General Bennett, commanding Australian Imperial Forces.**

stronghold of Singapore began on that day with air raids on British airfields and a simultaneous invasion of the Malay Peninsula to the north. The RAF was caught napping and by December 9 most of their planes had been disabled, destroying any hope of significant air support to the British forces.

The next day, torpedoes sank two British warships – *Prince of Wales* and *Repulse* – that had been sent north to prevent the landing of Japanese forces. On hearing the news Churchill noted: "I put the telephone down. I was thankful to be alone. In all the war I never received a more direct shock."

Meanwhile the Japanese troops, using light vehicles and bicycles for maximum speed, thundered southward through the difficult terrain of the peninsula with orders to take no prisoners that might slow them down.

The British had, in fact, anticipated an attack from the north and it had been recognized that the only way to prevent it was to secure a comprehensive defense of the Peninsula. However, they had completely underestimated the ferocity of the assault and had fatally under resourced the required defenses.

The Japanese swept southward and by January 31, 1942 Malaya fell. The Allied troops in the Peninsula had

■ ABOVE: **Winston Churchill.**

■ RIGHT: **The conference at which Singapore surrendered.**

■ BELOW: **Lietenant General Percival, seen here after liberation from a Japanese prison camp by American forces in Yokohama, September 12, 1945.**

been quickly routed and had retreated across the Kranji River to the island of Singapore, destroying the Johor-Singapore Causeway in their flight. By the next day, despite a spirited defense by Australian troops, the Japanese had the upper hand and the siege of Singapore began.

The island was now the target of continuous and devastating shelling. Meanwhile the British commander, Lieutenant General Arthur Percival, who now had the entire remaining Allied force under his control, spread his men thinly across the entire northern coast in the hope of stemming the enemy invasion. This was a mistake, as on February 8 the

Japanese sent 23,000 men across the water and punched a hole in the thin Allied line, spreading across the island like blood in sand.

They devastated everything before them and their treatment of military personnel and civilians alike was shocking and unprecedented. The captured, the wounded, those who surrendered, officials, doctors, and nurses were mercilessly murdered by the Japanese in their unstoppable onslaught.

On February 15, with 5,000 dead or wounded, Percival called for a ceasefire and ultimately surrendered his surviving force of nearly 80,000 men, leaving them to a brutal fate in the hands of an unmerciful enemy. The Japanese had lost about 4,500 men killed and wounded.

Churchill, who was at least partially to blame because of his political failure to resource a realistic defense, called the defeat:

"The worst disaster and largest capitulation in British history."

The Battle of Stalingrad

"Surrender is forbidden..."

That was the final message sent directly by Hitler to his commander on the Russian front, bogged down in his assault on Stalingrad in January 1943. The commander, General Friedrich Paulus, must have despaired as he read on – " ... the 6th army will hold their positions to the last man and the last round..." But perhaps even he, as he crunched through the snow and surveyed the bleak outlook through clouds of freezing breath in the biting cold, did not appreciate the full scale of the calamity that was about to follow the order. Over one million men had been thrown at Stalin's Russia and most of this force was now dead, wounded, or trapped. He could have withdrawn his forces before now, but, by Hitler's direct command, he had been prevented from doing so. His position was now untenable and, despite this last order, the surviving 90,000 German troops would surrender just a week later. Of these, only 6,000 would ever get home.

Paulus had been sent to take control of the oil fields in the Caucasus but had paused to take Stalingrad rather than leave the city

BELOW: Captured German soldiers, their uniforms tattered from the battle, making their way in the bitter cold through the ruins of Stalingrad.

OPPOSITE: Field Marshal Friedrich Paulus after the capitulation.

to his rear. On July 17, 1942 the Luftwaffe began to hurl destruction on Stalingrad in preparation for the ground assault by the 6th army supported by the 4th Panzer army, which took up a position north of the city on August 23.

The Russians were as determined not to allow Stalingrad to fall as were the Germans to take it, and they prepared to put up a massive resistance. Meanwhile their commander, General Georgy Zhukov, was hatching an ambitious plan to trap the Axis enemy. On September 13 the ground battle began with a huge assault by Paulus, and fierce continuous fighting through the streets followed. It was a vast and grim battle, with heavy casualties on both sides as parts of the city were taken and retaken in hand-to-hand fighting at enormous cost.

The scale of the opposing forces was almost unimaginable. Both sides had over one million men, while the Germans had over 10,000 artillery pieces to the Russians' 13,500. The troops under Paulus were assisted by 675 tanks, while Zhukov had nearly 900. In the skies above, each side had over 1,100 aircraft.

The carnage continued throughout October and November, but by November 19 Zhukov was ready to spring his trap. He had brought together six armies to encircle the city and, with most of the Germans still fighting in the streets, they were entirely surrounded. Even as the trap was closing, Paulus could have pulled out – but Hitler ordered him to stay. With terrible losses, below zero temperatures, and all of his supplies running low, by February Paulus had no option but to defy Hitler's command and surrender, with 91,000 of his men being taken prisoner. In all, the Germans suffered some 750,000 killed, wounded, or missing and their ability to defend their eastern front was forever damaged.

Hitler was full of rage at the shame of the defeat and stripped Paulus, whom he had expected to commit suicide, of his rank and honors. But had he agreed to any of the several requests from Paulus to withdraw while there was still time, his army in the east could have been saved. His tactical blunder created the turning point in World War II and left the eastern door open to the Russians, who would eventually pass through it and take Berlin.

Operation Market Garden

■ ABOVE: **General George S. Patton, left, with General Omar Bradley, center, and British General Bernard Montgomery, somewhere in Normandy, August 15, 1944.**

There is a famous blunder in Greek mythology that should serve as a lesson to the mere mortals of the modern world. Daedalus, a Cretan master craftsman, built two pairs of wings out of wax and feathers for himself and his son, Icarus, in order to escape imprisonment. He warned his son not to fly too close to the sun, but Icarus was too ambitious and soared upward, until the sun's heat melted his wings and he fell into the sea.

After the initial impetus of the D-Day offensive, the British commander, General Montgomery, was under huge pressure to come up with a decisive plan to punch the Allied attack into German territory and deliver a hammer blow to the enemy. Monty was used to success and, perhaps because of the pressure, he devised a scheme that was too ambitious and was ultimately doomed to failure.

His plan was to spearhead a narrow attack on to German soil from the Dutch/German border by rapidly taking eight bridges that would allow access across the matrix of rivers and canals that stood between his ground forces and the German heartland. To create the element of surprise he would drop 30,000 men by parachute and in gliders behind the German lines and secure the bridges so that the advancing ground troops could cross over into Germany.

With only days left before the attack, British intelligence obtained aerial photographs which suggested that two SS Panzer divisions were encamped near the bridge at Arnhem. In addition, the local German anti-aircraft defenses were now considered so strong that it was found necessary for the men to land seven miles away from their target and, at the same time, it was realized that there were too few planes to carry the airborne army all in one go and that it would take three days to complete the drop. Despite all of these damaging factors,

■ ABOVE: **Allied paratroopers entering one of the huge transports before taking off for the assault on German occupied Holland during Operation Market Garden, September 17, 1944.**

■ BELOW: **The bridge at Arnhem, showing, at the top, British troops and German armored vehicles.**

Monty decided to go ahead with the plan and the blunder of over ambition had been made.

On September 17, 1944 the huge airborne flotilla – some 500 gliders and 1,500 planes – took to the air and dropped its forces into the designated areas. On board, the US 101st Airborne Division were aiming at the crossings north west of Eindhoven, the US 82nd Airborne Division concentrating on the bridges at Grave and Nijmegen, and the British 1st Airborne Division landing closer to Arnhem – the final bridge in the plan. They flew over the British XXX Corps – a ground force of some 50,000 men – that would march on Arnhem and link up with the advance force within 48 hours. Unfortunately, very little worked to plan.

The US troops met with mixed success, finding some of the bridges already blown before their arrival. Meanwhile strong German resistance delayed the advance of the ground troops along the narrow Eindhoven to Arnhem road.

As soon as they landed the British airborne troops ran into problems, as it was found that their radio communications were faulty. When they finally reached the bridge at Arnhem they faced massive resistance from a crack Panzer force and took up positions in the buildings close to the north end of the bridge. Without the expected reinforcements, here they had to remain under constant and heavy fire.

XXX Corps linked up with US forces at the Nijmegen Bridge and finally took it – but only after a very costly river crossing in which great numbers of men were lost. Although the route to Arnhem was now open to them, it would be four days before the advance British troops were to be supported.

The 1st Airborne Division, holed up in houses clustered around the bridge at Arnhem, had no effective defense against the German tanks that now set about systematically destroying the buildings one by one. Suffering terrible casualties they were forced to withdraw. Meanwhile, on the other side of the river, the men of XXX Corps finally arrived, but were unable to cross. General Horrocks, commanding, ordered the evacuation of the paratroops on the north side, but from the large force only 2,500 finally made the crossing. They left 1,500 dead and over 6,500 wounded and prisoners.

Operation Market Garden was a bold, but flawed, plan fatally damaged by poor intelligence but, ultimately, by over ambition.

BELOW: American tanks cross the bridge at Nijmegen, Holland, captured intact, on November 24, 1944, when the town fell to the advancing US forces.

Operation Eagle Claw

During the ongoing tensions between the USA and the Islamic revolution within a number of Middle Eastern countries in the late 1970s and early 1980s, Iranian students took hostage 52 American citizens – despite their diplomatic immunity – and held them prisoner in the US Embassy in Tehran. This was a slap in the face for America and the American people were outraged.

In a world used to "smart" warfare and secret operations where highly trained undercover forces could swoop to glory, Jimmy Carter's US government was under pressure to produce a speedy and decisive result to the crisis. Politically, to do nothing was not an option and, with an up-coming election, Carter wanted a resounding American victory. Within days he ordered a rescue mission, with the name of "Operation Eagle Claw."

The resulting plan required the establishment of a ground base within Iranian territory, from which a helicopter assault on the embassy

■ ABOVE: A representative of the Iranian students holds up a portrait of one of the blindfolded hostages during a press conference at the US Embassy in Tehran, November 5, 1979.

■ RIGHT: President Jimmy Carter tenses his lips, as he faces reporters at the White House in Washington on November 28, 1979, to a comment regarding the latest situation at the US Embassy in Tehran.

could be launched. This base, called Desert One, was intended to receive six supply aircraft carrying men, equipment, and fuel and also to become the base for a minimum of six RH-53 navy helicopters for the actual rescue in Tehran. The helicopters would later move on to Desert Two, from where the embassy would be attacked.

While in fact only four helicopters were necessary for the final assault on the embassy, it was deemed sensible that at least six operational machines should be sent and, crucially, it was decided that, should the number of operational helicopters fall below six, the mission would be aborted. In the event, eight helicopters were sent to Desert One. Three weeks before the operation, Desert One was surveyed by Major John Carney Jr. and declared fit for purpose. During his visit the ground was composed of hard-packed sand… but sandstorms were to alter the terrain in the forthcoming weeks.

■ **ABOVE: President Jimmy Carter speaks to the American people on nationwide television from the White House in Washington April 25, 1980, to brief them on the aborted attempt to rescue the US hostages in Tehran.**

There was some early damage with one of the first aircraft to be sent, but ultimately the stage was set and the eight helicopters – coded Bluebeard one to eight – took off for Desert One from the aircraft carrier USS *Nimitz*. It was now that the plan began to unravel.

Sand is a fickle substance and moves in mysterious ways. Within a particular type of air movement following a storm, known as a haboob, very fine sand particles hover in the air in an almost liquid state. The American force had not foreseen this condition and it had a devastating effect upon the operation.

As the eight Bluebeard choppers crossed the desert toward Desert One, number six developed problems and was grounded and abandoned, its crew being taken up by Bluebeard eight, while Bluebeard five was forced to return to the *Nimitz* with engine problems. Bluebeard two arrived at Desert One, but was severely damaged by the sand and could not continue with the mission. Now, with only five helicopters left in active service and with fears of further problems should they be used, the recommendation was made to abort the mission. Within two hours President Carter approved the abort.

This dismal failure would have been bad enough under the subsequent spotlight of the world's media, but worse was to follow. The chaos, disruption, and delays had caused further logistical problems – including lack of fuel – which required various maneuvers in the sand-heavy air. Bluebeard three was stationed directly behind one of the EC-130 transports and needed to move to assist in the refueling of Bluebeard four. As the helicopter fired up, the rotor blades churned up a dense cloud of sand and, in the ensuing blind confusion, it crashed into the transport plane.

There was an explosion followed by a fire and eight American servicemen died, with two more badly wounded. Defeated and demoralized the remaining US troops made a frantic evacuation, leaving various equipment and five helicopters to their Iranian foe.

Carter lost the election.